101 Ways to Save Money in a Recession

101 Ways to Save Money in a Recession

Tom Winnifrith

Beautiful
Books

Beautiful Books Limited
36-38 Glasshouse Street
London W1B 5DL

www.beautiful-books.co.uk

ISBN 9781907616198

9 8 7 6 5 4 3 2 1

Printed in the UK by CPI Mackays, Chatham ME5 8TD.

Dedicated to the one and only
Olivia Winnifrith,
who now needs to persuade her Grandfather
to write a What Happened Next? *book and to*
her scholarly Grandfather for being an example to
us all and, in advance, for writing
What Happened Next?.

Contents

Introduction

22. Never buy white shirts for work.
23. Check the pressure on your car tyres.
24. Always use the recommended grade of motor oil to save on petrol costs.
25. And drive sensibly to save petrol.
26. Buy petrol at at the cheapest location.
27. Do not assume that the AA or RAC are the best value for breakdown cover.
28. If you have a home computer, register with www.skype.com to make all your phone calls.
29. Sticking with the phone theme – do you really need the mobile you have?
30. Cut your life insurance costs.
31. Never go for 3-for-2 offers at supermarkets and try to resist BOGOF (Buy One Get One Free).
32. While on the subject of supermarkets, if you have to visit, go half an hour before they shut.
33. Save money on herbs.
34. Cut your heating bills at a stroke.
35. General electricity bills can also be slashed.
36. Do not pay to get your car washed.
37. Swap your skills for other people's skills and save cash.
38. Go to free events and TV shows.
39. Think about changing your utility supplier.
40. Invest in three plastic piggy banks (99p each at discount stores) and position them around the house.
41. Repay your mortgage early.
42. Never buy designer labels.
43. You cannot live without designer labels? Okay, buy second hand.
44. If you insist on going to the cinema check out the special offers.
45. Use supermarkets not corner stores.
46. Take out redundancy insurance now. Or not at all.
47. Get free dental treatment.
48. Do not buy adult members of your extended family Christmas presents.
49. Take a mature approach to your partner's gift.

50. Cut down on or cut out after work drinks.
51. Pay your insurance premiums in one go, not by monthly payments.
52. Check all your bank statements each month.
53. Never pay to take cash out of a cash point machine or ATM.
54. Never buy a new car, whatever generous terms the motor dealer offers you.
55. Always use the sales to do your shopping, but shop sensibly.
56. But do not buy in the sales what you do not need!
57. Do not sign up to any get-rich schemes involving courses on anything from stock market success to sports betting or new franchise opportunities.
58. On the other hand, always enter free competitions.
59. Sign up to take part in online market research.
60. Make sure that you have a loyalty card for each supermarket you use.
61. Never buy an additional extended warranty on an electrical product.
62. Book your flights early.
63. If you are going on a short-haul or even medium-haul flight, take a packed lunch.
64. If you are planning to drive to the airport, think well in advance about where you will park.
65. Don't buy a turkey at Christmas.
66. Recycle your Christmas tree.
67. Always use price comparison websites.
68. Start a pension as soon as you begin work.
69. Grandparents should, for Christmas presents, always consider handing down family momentos, the family silver or other treasured possessions.
70. If you have a garden, try growing some of your own food.
71. Do NOT join a gym after Christmas because you feel fat.
72. If hint number 71 comes too late for you, quit your gym now.
73. When you use a washing machine, use it on the lowest heat.
74. Do not bother to use extra energy with a spin dry programme.
75. Flog your unwanted possessions on eBay.

76. When you are going abroad, let your friends know and ask them to text rather than phone.

77. When the weather starts to get colder (around August 29th here in the Isle of Man) do not automatically turn up the heating.

78. Do not use the scoops provided by manufacturers of detergents for your washing machine.

79. Do not boil a full kettle.

80. If you shop online, use promotional codes.

81. Do not buy ready made meals.

82. Cut down on the meat.

83. Do not let food go off.

84. Make some money out of those old Cliff Richard and Brotherhood of Man CDs.

85. You can also realise cash for old mobile phones.

86. Complete and prepare to submit your tax return as soon as possible.

87. If your pet passes away, don't replace him/her/it.

88. Cut out or cut down on the number of times you eat out.

89. Do not use taxis ever – use public transport.

90. Use the January sales to buy kids' birthday party presents in advance.

91. If you are truly desperate for cash, then loan your body to medical science.

92. If you have cleared all your debts and are ready to save, use an ISA (and Individual Savings Allowance).

93. Mr Muscle, Vim and all those expensive sprays and squeezy bottles packed full of chemicals for cleaning your house are a complete waste of money.

94. Cut down on the number of TV channels you pay for on Sky.

95. You can get extra entertainment for free at your local library.

96. Get your hair cut for free.

97. Do not bother with a hotel when going on holiday.

98. Stop using 0870 or 0871 numbers.

99. Stop buying bottled water.

100. Do not pay bills late.

101. Stop buying lottery tickets.

Introduction

Are we in a recession? Or a depression? Do we face a double dip? Ask 12 economists and the only thing you know for sure is that you will get 12 different answers. Possibly more as a couple of the experts will change their mind before the exercise is complete.

What we 'non experts' can say for sure is that life for the next few years will be pretty tough. The Government has to cut its spending and – not to put too fine a point on it – that means sacking vast numbers of its employees. This is unlikely to do much to boost the housing market and consumer spending since it will not be accompanied by any meaningful tax cuts. So for you and me that means that we face several years when job insecurity will be an ever present feature of our lives – indeed, we may well face spells between jobs. If we dodge the P45s successfully then the wage increases we will be offered will not be that great. Why should employers compete to retain labour by paying us more when there are eight million economically inactive Britons of working age who are likely to be forced to seek gainful employment?

If it sounds pretty grim I am sorry. If you wish to bury your head in the sand and carry on spending like a deranged lottery winner that is your prerogative but I would advise against it. It would be more sensible to save money where you can – without pain – because in tough times those with money will at the very least survive and at best, flourish as they pick up bargains, be that houses, shares or season tickets at their favoured football club, from distressed sellers. What follows are 101 ways to save money in a recession. Some you may regard as frivolous but they will save you money none the less. Others could transform your life. As I start a new life in a new country (okay, the Isle of Man), contemplating how I could save a few pounds here and there, I came up with 101 ways to transform my finances. I doubt I shall be disciplined enough to adopt half of them but even so, it is not hard to make a material impact on your disposable income. And that cannot be a bad thing whatever the state of the economy.

But before we start the 101 handy hints, a quick note on compounding. If you save £100 a year over 20 years, what do you think that is worth? £2000? Oh no. The answer is £3,741.93, or perhaps it is £6,300.25. It is certainly not £2,000. That is down to the principle of compounding. My assumption is that the £100 you save each year will be invested and will earn a return. Say it is 5%: after one year you will have £105. And that £105 will next year be worth £105 x 1.05, and so on. If we assume that your £100 earns a 5% return each year then £100 saved each year will be worth £3,741.93 at the end of 20 years. If we use a 10% assumption it will be worth £6,300.25.

I will show how most homeowners can ensure a tax free return of at least 5% later on. But compounding is the key to all savings and indeed all investments. Never forget it.

1

Give up smoking
(except in some cases where you should
carry on for a couple more years).

It is a filthy habit which makes you smell disgusting and will kill you. We all know that but heck, it is fun. Unfortunately it is also incredibly costly. The last time I bought a packet of 20 (two hours ago) I walked out of the shop £6.46 poorer. Now assume that you buy one packet a day, then each year you are spending £2,357.90 on cigarettes. Throw in a bit for lighters and matches and shall we say £2,370 a year. Think what you could do with that much spare cash! But the figure gets more daunting if you assume that you can quit for 20 years. If you compound that saving at just 5%, by quitting today you will be £82,284.63 better off. Over 25 years the total saving becomes £118,768.90. To put that into perspective that is enough to clear 90% of the average mortgage in the UK today.

2

Carry on smoking if you are less than 10 years from retirement (and have a pension).

This may sound like lunacy but if you are within 10 years of retirement you should carry on smoking, albeit cut down to 10 a day and plan to give up the day after you retire. This is because when you retire your pension will be used to buy an annuity – essentially a bond which pays out an annual return. The insurance companies pay out a return based on how long they expect you to live and if you have been a smoker for the preceeding 10 years (even at 10 a day) they reckon that you will carry on smoking and that you will probably die sooner as a result. Hence they will give you up to 25% more as an annual return on that annuity because they know they will be shelling out for a shorter period. So aged 50, if you are still smoking, cut down to 10 a day (10 a day rather than 20 a day will over 10 years on a compounded basis save you £15,650.04), bag a 25% increase in your annuity and then stop smoking altogether the next day.

3

Buy your Christmas cards, crackers and wrapping paper in January.

Designs on Christmas cards and wrapping paper never change. Fat Santas, snowmen, robins, snowflakes, angels, the baby Jesus and the three wise men: the cast never changes. The jokes in Christmas crackers weren't that funny 50 years ago when they were first created – they don't change either. And like Advent Calendars (except for those with chocolates inside) they can be stored away in a dry and safe place for 12 months.

But retailers are just desperate to get rid of all their Christmas stock in January. Indeed, by Christmas Eve it is all pretty much useless. For them it is dead money once the Happy Holiday season is over – just an item that has to be moved into storage where it takes up space and cannot be turned into cash for another 11 months. And for that reason they will almost give such items away, slashing prices by 50, 60 or 70% as December draws to a close. So spend £50 just after this Christmas on all the cards, wrapping paper, tinsel, crackers, Advent Calendars you will use next Christmas and you should be saving £50 to £100.

4

Better still, think cleverly about Christmas cards.

The cheapest option is to just send an e-card by email. But a) not everyone is on email and b) they are very impersonal and you cannot stick them up around the house to make it feel as if Christmas is almost upon us. Call me a traditionalist old bore but I hate e-cards. So instead, use the Christmas cards you received last year which will all follow a standard format of a picture on the front with a blank space behind it and a message on page three with some printing on the back of page four. Simply cut them in half and use the first two pages as a Christmas postcard to your nearest and dearest this year. There is no need for an envelope, just a low cost stamp and a message on the back. Cheap and very environmentally friendly to boot. And remember to post Christmas cards early in December so that you can post second class rather than first and still ensure that they arrive on time.

5

Do the weekly grocery shop online.

This has two advantages. The most obvious is that if you have already written your shopping list – something that you should always do and always stick to – the temptation to add additional items as you wander down the aisles is greatly reduced. The second is that you avoid using your car which – with petrol at 120p a litre – is just a very expensive exercise.

6

Save and make money on your holidays.

Three handy tips in one. Firstly, never buy foreign currency at the airport – the service may be flagged as 'no cost' but the exchange rates you are offered are very poor. You will save at least 10% by pre-ordering cash from your bank. Some debit cards (not all) should be used simply to take cash from an ATM while abroad. Other debit cards will charge you an additional fee per transaction when abroad. To find out which cards you should or should not use when going abroad on holiday go to **www.travelmoneymax.com**.

When going on holiday in the EU remember to get an EHIC. This free card entitles you to free or discounted treatment in state run EU hospitals. The alternative can be very costly. You can get full details at **www.ehic.org.uk**.

And, finally, if you are a smoker remember that you can bring home as many cigarettes as you wish from abroad as long as they are for personal use. HMRC reckon that bringing home fewer than 3,200 cigarettes (160 packs) will not see questions asked. Given that cigarettes are markedly cheaper in most places than the UK it pays to stock up. If you are a non smoker do a deal with a mate who is addicted. Buy him 160 packs and split the savings with him. I should note that this is illegal since your cigarettes are not for personal use, but frankly who is going to find out? You can cut similar deals on alcohol if you wish.

7

And when you get home, get paid to review your holiday.

No, really. Well, I cannot believe that this will work for most of us but when you get home go to **www.simon-seeks.com** to write up your holiday. If other viewers of this website (set up by Simon Nixon who founded Moneysupermarket.com) rate your piece highly you will start to get paid for it. I suspect that two weeks in Benidorm won't earn you anything but if you review a truly fascinating place where no-one ever goes, like the Isle of Man where I live, then you might earn the odd penny.

8

Get credit cards to provide you with working capital at no cost.

Credit cards charge very high rates of interest (well into double digits even today) and they are highly profitable because most people actually pay that interest. This is high cost debt and should be avoided like the plague by the prudent saver. But if you clear your balance at the end of every month you pay no interest at all. As such, credit cards can be used to fund all your spending until payday when you clear the outstanding balance and start again. But beware, if you fail to make a monthly payment in full you start getting clobbered with interest. So if, like me, you are not disciplined or organised enough to ensure you meet your bills in full every month, do yourself a favour and cut up your credit cards as they will become an expensive vice. Indeed, you must clear any credit card debt you do have AT ONCE. This is really very serious advice.

Let us say that you had a credit card debt of £3,300 at an interest rate of 15% (which even today is not unusual), that will over three years cost you £817.50 in interest. Ouch. Clear that any way you can. Perhaps if you have spare equity in your house you might extend your mortgage by £3,300 and if you are paying 5%

on your mortgage (not unrealistic) your interest costs over 3 years will be just £261.25 – so you are £556.25 better off. Always remember that credit card debt is financially lethal. Do whatever you can to avoid it.

9

Take a packed lunch and thermos flask to work.

What does it cost to buy one latte and a sandwich from Starbucks each working day? You won't be getting much change from £6. Even your local coffee store is going to take you down for a fiver. So each working year your use of Starbucks will set you back £1,440. That is great news for shareholders in Starbucks since it will be earning a gross margin of at least 60% on your custom but is it really that great for you? Now, how about you invest in a thermos and a plastic lunch box? Thereafter you can take your own coffee to work (cost per day with milk, 20p) and make a packed lunch with a couple of sandwiches (probably healthier than the Starbucks offering) with a couple of pieces of fruit for less than £1.30 a day. Not only will you be eating more healthy food but your net saving over the course of a working year amounts to £1,080.

Now, are you feeling richer already? We have another 92 money saving tips to go. We've only just *started* to save.

10

Milk the benefits system.

Look, there are folks out there a lot less deserving than you who are doing it every day, so while the system is clearly flawed, use it if you can. For reasons which I cannot quite understand, families earning up to £66,000 a year can still be entitled to State assistance in the UK. Check out what you can claim at **www.turn2us.org.uk**.

11

Install a water meter
(unless you have an enormous family or
keep an elephant in the back garden).

In almost all circumstances you will not be charged for
the installation. The fact is that water bills are set in
relation to the rateable value of your house. So if you
live in a large house you will pay more than if you live
in a small house. Overall, the water companies reckon
it averages out and they make a profit on water supply.
But if you are a low water user – because no-one is in
the house during the day as they are at work, or there
are just one or two people in a big house or, perhaps, if
your family has some sort of aversion to basic personal
hygiene – then you are probably paying too much and
should get a meter.

And the odd thing is that when you cease to view water
as free, you actually start to notice how much you use.
You really pack that washing machine and showers rather
than baths become an automatic choice. Put a brick in
the cistern for your loo and slash the amount used on
each flush. You can get more advice on this no-brainer
for many people at **www.uswitch.com**.

12

If you have time on your hands and are looking for that little bit of extra work there are many alternative ways of making a few pounds.

Register to be a film extra at **www.filmextras.co.uk** or **www.2020casting.com**. My father got recruited in a pub to be an extra in the truly awful recent remake of *Brideshead Revisited*. They were looking for ageing eccentric-looking old men to appear as ageing eccentric academic types in the Oxford scenes. This is type-casting, as my father *is* an ageing eccentric academic and looks the part. I cannot say that I caught his 50 nanoseconds of screen glory but he earned £50 and a free lunch. I think I have just outed him to the taxman. I suspect others might escape that particular net.

13

Alternatively, get into pet sitting.

Register at **www.platinumpetcare.co.uk** to look after other people's pets when they want a cat- or dog-free weekend. When I am away from home it is a condition of employment that my staff have to take it in turns to come and feed and talk to Kitosh, my cat. So I have no need of a cat minder and indeed have the added pleasure of making my compliance officer Nick Woolard suffer once every couple of months, as he cannot escape the Kitosh rota and is horribly allergic to cats. It is just part of his job. But other folks do not have a Nick to torture and so need outside help, since leaving cats and dogs in a cat or dog sanctuary is both traumatic for your pet and also horribly expensive. If you like pets why not earn a few pounds talking to a cat for a weekend?

And finally, in the alternative jobs section, why not get paid for listening to music?

Visit **www.slicethepie.com** and if you can understand the instructions (which I admit that I could not) you earn 5p for listening to a track and rating it. Okay, that works out at probably only 60p an hour but if you have nothing else to do and you truly love music it is better for your finances than just sitting at home watching Trisha.

15

Insulate your loft.

The aim of home improvements is simple: make the house feel warmer as you lose less heat to the outside world so that you can turn down your heaters. You save money and the UK does its bit to help stop global warming. The key to your return is grants. The UK Government is, as you know, so awash with cash that it can afford to fund hair removal treatments for sex change patients on the NHS and to pay for disabled people to go to Amsterdam to have sex with prostitutes. It is also, in this spirit of largesse, keen to give you a grant of up to 100% – whatever your income – to have your loft insulated. It is possible that in the future Government spending may be cut and while vital services (like the hair removal therapy) will no doubt escape the Chancellor's knife, the insulation grants may not last forever. So apply while you can. But even without a grant, loft insulation makes sense, as the average payback in terms of reduced heating bills is between three and six years and insulation should last for at least 40 years. So you will make a good return on your investment. Loft insulation should also add a bit to the price of your house should you sell.

16

Do not install double glazing.

It is an appalling waste of money (whatever the salesmen say). The type of double glazing you buy varies greatly in cost from £500 to £4,000 for a typical home. It will save heat but only a minimal amount and you cannot get a grant for this work. So the payback period will range from 30 (on secondary double glazing at £500) to 80 years (on the full monty). The odds are, therefore, that if you go for full double glazing you will not see any payback in your lifetime. Unless that is new double glazing for your tortoise house. Even the 30-year payback does not sound that great – it is the equivalent of a 2.3% compounded rate of return per annum. Now I am sure we can do better than that, can we not?

17

From home to abroad.

Do not automatically renew annual travel insurance unless you are about to go away. Let it lapse until the next time you are going to go away. Why pay for months of cover that you do not actually need? Indeed, there is a case for not going away at all. I always find that after a trip away I am exhausted by all the travel and then have the stress of catching up on all the work I missed and I am much worse off as a result. Opt for a 'staycation' where you take time off work, switch off your PC and phone and just rest at home. Read a few books. Enjoy all the local attractions that you never get around to visiting. It took me eight years of living in London to go to the Tower of London. After 20 years in London I had still not visited Kew Gardens, The Tate, Crystal Palace, the London Barrier and so much more. How much stress and money would I have saved with a London staycation rather than yet another exhausting trek out to France?

18

Never try to save until you are debt free.

This is one of life's golden rules but one that most of us break at one time or another. If you have an over-draft or credit card debt you will almost certainly be paying interest at a rate of 10%-20%. If you save (even in a tax-free wrapper such as an ISA) you will over the long run probably only generate single digit returns. Warren Buffet may manage 23% per annum but that is why we have all heard of him. The odds are that you will not get anywhere near that level. So why risk your capital on an investment product which will only make you 7% when you are paying 15% on borrowed money? It is a surefire way to waste cash. Only when you have cleared your debts should you start to save.

19

Try to get some money back from the banks for all those snotty letters they sent you telling you that you were overdrawn or that a cheque had bounced.

The banks have historically thought it fair to charge you up to £30 for sending such an (automated) letter when the cost to the bank of sending such an (automated) letter was less than a quid. A number of legal rulings in the past two years made it clear that the banks were quite simply profiteering, ripping off its customers in order to pay bank mega-bonuses. And as such you can now complain and get compensation. There is a tortuous official process to go through which is detailed at **www. thisismoney.co.uk/bankcharges** but it is, frankly, all a bit of a pain. An alternative route is simply to contact your bank manager in writing or – if you can find him – face to face, and produce your statements (things you should always keep) showing how many times you have been ripped off. The bank can wriggle, prevaricate and delay but ultimately it knows it has to pay. In my case my manager made me an offer which was not as much as I could have gone for but I could not be bothered to haggle and just accepted. After all, it is not every day that your bank actually gives you money, is it?

20

Cut down on your travel-to-work costs and lose some weight while you are at it.

If you live in London, why not get off the tube one station early – especially if you 'save a zone' – and walk the last mile or so? If you catch a train to work, get off a station early. The savings may be tiny but they add up. Go one stage further and use a bicycle – certainly if you work in London and can avoid the prohibitive costs of public transport. As it happens employers can pay for employees to buy bikes as a tax deductible expense so why not lobby your boss to pay for you to save money? If you insist on using public transport in London to get to work, buy an Oystercard as it does work out materially cheaper than buying individual tickets for the tube and bus.

21

Buy own brand goods not branded equivalents when at the supermarket.

This really is an easy way to slash your shopping bills. What is the difference between Tesco/Asda/Sainsbury's baked beans and those produced by Heinz? Answer: the label. Sure, there might be marginally different ingredients but you and your family simply will not notice the change. Beanz does NOT mean Heinz. And the price savings are vast. At Tesco (but the same sort of thing is true at the Co-Op, Asda, Sainsbury, etc) a 420-gram tin of organic baked beans (own label) costs 40p. A 415-gram tin of Heinz organic beans costs 76p. Effectively, Tesco's own-label product is — bean for bean — almost 50% cheaper. And the same is true for a whole range of goods. On a weekly shop of £60 you can easily save £15 by buying own-brand only — that works out at £780 a year.

22

Never buy white shirts for work.

Even if you do not stain them with spillage – which I always do – it is only a matter of time before they go off-colour. The bottom line is that – if you care about your appearance – they have a shorter useful working life than coloured shirts. However, when those white shirts you so unwisely bought before reading this book do start to go a little grey, do not panic. Invest in a bottle of blue dye or maybe pink dye, which should set you back no more than a couple of pounds, dye the shirts carefully and you have (almost) brand new shirts. And remember that, even after a shirt really goes dreadfully off-colour or gets torn, its useful life is not at an end. Cut it up to use as household dusters or use bits of it to tie across your Christmas puddings (when you make your own rather than buying in, naturally) at Christmas time.

23

Check the pressure on your car tyres.

Not only does this improve car safety but it actually reduces the cost of motoring. It does this in two ways. Firstly, maintaining tyres at the correct pressure will increase the working life of a tyre and make it less vulnerable to punctures. You probably won't notice that too much, so just view that as a hidden benefit. More tangible is that you can increase the fuel efficiency of your car by doing so, by up to 3.3%. When it costs £60 to fill up your tank you are talking about a saving of £2 a refill for this. The actual statistic is that under-inflated tires reduce petrol mileage efficiency by around 0.3% for ever one psi drop in pressure. The correct tyre pressure for your car is usually found on a sticker in the driver's side door jamb or the glove box and in your owner's manual. Do not use the maximum pressure printed on the tyre's inner rim.

Always use the recommended grade of motor oil to save on petrol costs.

You can improve your petrol mileage efficiency by 1-2% by using the manufacturer's recommended grade of motor oil. For example, using 10W-30 motor oil in an engine designed to use 5W-30 can lower your petrol mileage by 1-2 percent. Using 5W-30 in an engine designed for 5W-20 can lower your petrol mileage by 1-1.5 percent. Also, look for motor oil that says 'Energy Conserving' on the API performance symbol to be sure it contains friction-reducing additives. Now, 1% to 2% may not sound like a lot but when you are paying £60 to fill a tank with petrol the saving is 60p-£1.20. It all adds up.

25

And drive sensibly to save petrol.

Aggressive driving (speeding, rapid acceleration and braking) simply wastes petrol. It can lower your miles per gallon or litre by up to 33% at motorway speeds and by around 5% driving around the city. Driving at above-optimum speed also wastes petrol. As the owner of a fast car living on an island where some roads have 'unrestricted' speeds (i.e. no speed limits at all) this is not what I want to hear but for every 5 miles per hour that I drive at above 60 miles per hour I am increasing the rate that I burn petrol by up to 8%.

While we are on the subject of fuel conservation, how much excess clutter is there in your car? The last time I looked in mine there were several blankets, a stack of books and various other items that I certainly won't be using this summer. The weight of these items adds up and reduces fuel efficiency. As a rule of thumb, for a normal car, each additional 3.5 stone in the car cuts fuel efficiency by around 1%. So if I could stick to a diet that worked I could cut the costs of refilling my tank by an effective 60p!

You are now almost a quarter of the way through this book. By now, you must have spotted at least two or three ways to make you richer (or at least less poor). Do not worry, there are another 76 handy hints to change your financial circumstances still to come.

Buy petrol at at the cheapest location.

If you are driving back from the continent, that normally means any service station more than 50 miles from Calais. If you are in the United Kingdom the variation in prices between different service stations can be vast. Check out the cheapest deals near to you at **www.petrolprices.com** but – this should go without saying – do not drive 100 miles just to save 3p per litre, as it is not worth it. Only use local garages but use the cheapest.

Do not assume that the AA or RAC are the best value for breakdown cover.

Most of us do use one of these dominant services but there is no real skill in going out to fix or tow away a broken car. It is not a magic formula. There are other national providers and it pays to shop around on the Internet. All will provide rescues throughout the UK. It goes without saying that you should not wait until you break down to apply for cover as this will prove rather expensive. Use **www.comparenow.com/insurance/breakdown-cover** to check out the best deals that apply to you where you live and for your type of car.

28

If you have a home computer, register with www.skype.com to make all your phone calls.

Ensure that your friends and family – especially if they live abroad – are also on Skype, then start calling. It is absolutely free with no standing charge. You can also make video calls at no charge. The sound quality is occasionally a little patchy and video quality is even more variable but it is improving all the time. And it's absolutely free. As I write there are 18.7 million people around the world online and on Skype who I could chat to or video conference without it costing me a cent. Unfortunately I appear to know only six of them and I have no real desire to talk to any of them. But on average I make around two personal calls a day on skype of which one will be abroad so it is probably saving me at least £1 a day.

29

Sticking with the phone theme – do you really need the mobile you have?

I am on the phone all day. I am a high user so, for me, pay-as-you-go just does not stack up. But my ageing father uses his mobile about once a month when he can find someone to explain to him how it works. He has a similar package to me and is just burning cash. Why should he pay £50 a month for calls he will never make and texts which he will never ever use? He should purchase a pay-as-you-go mobile for as little as £30 and then purchase top-ups whenever he needs to (i.e. once in a blue moon). This is perhaps an extreme example of money blown on mobile phones but why not check your bills for the last three months (or keep a diary of your phone usage) to see exactly what your patterns of use are in terms of texts, domestic phone calls and international calls – then see whether the package you have is actually the one that is most suitable for you.

30

Cut your life insurance costs.

The odds are that you took out your policy when you took out a mortgage. The cost of that insurance was almost certainly the last thing on your mind – you just wished to get another box ticked on that long list of things to do. Perhaps your bank helpfully introduced you to an insurance company it owned which would make life so much simpler for you? The odds are that even if your circumstances have not changed, if you shopped around you could now find cheaper cover, possibly saving a couple of quid a week, even if your circumstances remain unaltered. But maybe you are onto a double win. My life insurance was taken out when I was a smoker and thus the actuaries stated that I was at a higher risk of pegging it so my cover cost me more than had I not been a smoker. Now when I give up smoking shortly – as I plan to do almost every week, for the reasons outlined 29 suggestions ago – then after a couple of years of clean living I will fall into a different actuarial risk category. Perhaps you have already quit smoking, lost a stack of weight or taken up hill walking since you took out life insurance. In which case it is worth checking if you can get a new policy offering the same cover for less.

31

Never go for 3-for-2 offers at supermarkets and try to resist BOGOF (Buy One Get One Free).

The odds are that you only really need one of any item, so you may reduce you average cost of purchase by going for a 3-for-2 but will you actually use all of that product? How many times have you got three packs of Clementines when you only really needed or wanted one for Christmas? By January, your fruit bowl is stacked with slightly rotting Clementines.

As for the BOGOF: the aim of this is to tempt you to make an impulse purchase of something you do not really want. As such, in giving in to the cunning marketing ploy of supermarkets (who will still make money by selling 2-for-1) you have parted with cash you did not need or really want to spend. That cash should be used for more useful purposes.

32

While on the subject of supermarkets, if you have to visit, go half an hour before they shut.

You will often find items discounted as they approach their sell-by dates and the stores just have to shift them. Obviously, do not buy what you do not need and what is not on your carefully prepared shopping list, but you might just save a few pounds on some items.

33

Save money on herbs.

Okay, this is small fry but buy fresh herbs rather than the packaged supermarket variety. Better still, these plants can be grown from seed in pots on your window sill, so anyone can grow them wherever they live in a tower block in Hackney or Osama's cave in Bora Bora. You do not need green fingers. Even I can manage it. Should you insist on buying fresh herbs rather than growing your own, you can keep them fresh for several weeks by wrapping them in damp (but not wet) kitchen towels and putting them in the fridge.

34

Cut your heating bills at a stroke.

Firstly try turning down the thermostat in your house. Move it down by one degree and I bet you that you will not notice a jot. But you will save around £10 a year on your bills. A couple of weeks later move it down by another degree and the savings double. What temperature do you have your domestic water heater set at? Do you really need to be scalded by hot water when you have a bath (or a shower — which is far more energy- and water-efficient?) No. Turn the water heater down to 60 degrees centigrade and you should be saving £15-20 a year. Meanwhile, keep the house warmer by closing the curtains as the afternoon draws to a close. And stop heat from escaping from your hot water tank by installing a jacket — it will cost you £10 but save you £15 a year. Insulating your hot water pipes will cost around £1 a yard but should save another £10-15 a year. That is a fairly rapid payback.

35

General electricity bills can also be slashed.

The simplest way is by changing your light bulbs to energy-saving light bulbs. These cost £4-8 each so are far more expensive than a normal light bulb but they last eight times longer than a normal higher watt bulb and they use only 25% of the power. As such the installation of one energy saving light bulb can save you up to £70 over its lifetime. Now, I bet your parents told you to switch off light bulbs to save money. They were correct. Leaving two normal light-bulbs on for two hours will cost you about 3p. Okay, that does not sound like a lot but if you think of how many times you leave lights on at night which you could have switched off or leave lights on during the day when you are out…it all adds up. My biggest offence in this category is leaving my laptop on all night so that I do not have to switch it back on and re-enter keywords to log on in the morning. This is criminal. Leaving my PC on overnight wastes enough money to microwave six meals. (Not that those meals come from Delia, you understand, or will understand after reading point 81.) While we are on the subject, turn your microwave off at the socket when not using it – otherwise it will simply be the most expensive-to-run digital clock you will ever own.

36

Do not pay to get your car washed.

I know that it is far simpler to go to a drive-through car wash and hand over your keys to a bunch of men in baseball caps than to do it yourself but it is a consummate waste of your cash. If you have kids, make them earn their pocket money (a useful training for later life) by washing your car once a week – while they are about it, they can tidy the house, do the washing up, etc. Okay, so the kids refuse. Get out a bucket and some soapy water and do it yourself. It will not take more than 20 minutes and the saving has to be £10-15. If you avoid a monthly visit to the carwash then your annual saving is £120-180. And that ignores the cost of driving to and from the carwash which – with petrol where it is – is unlikely to be insignificant.

37

Swap your skills for other people's skills and save cash.

I can just about change a light bulb and switch a fuse in a plug. And that is where my DIY skills come to an end. But I am a dab hand in the garden. So why don't I agree to keep the garden of some old chap who is too crocked to use a spade and fork but who can help me to get my central heating going again — something I need to do urgently ahead of the start of the Manx winter on about August 29th. This is the idea behind LETS (Local Exchange Trading Schemes), details of which can be found at **www.letslinkuk.net** — there are around 40,000 Brits already involved in such schemes, including my stepmother (see hint 45 below). It is tempting to parody such schemes as involving a stack of '60s children who can swap skills in Rekhi therapy for advice on spiritual healing or Feng Shui but that is a bit unfair (although not totally unfair). If you have a practical skill to offer, you will probably find your services in demand in a local LETS group — but you will also find a number of other services (including a vast number of spiritual advisers) on offer. The LETS network is widespread so there should be a group near you, although the Isle of Man seems to have survived without one so far.

38

Go to free events and TV shows.

Yes you can. To see listings of carnivals, fiestas, balloon tournaments, you name it, which are happening throughout the UK go to **www.free-events.co.uk** – for a family day out at zero cost. Remember to take a packed lunch as takeaway food at most events is a) expensive, b) disgusting and c) more likely to give you food poisoning than your average packed lunch. Or how about entertaining the kids by watching a TV show being filmed? Heck, for some of the offerings on BBC3 you turning up in the studio with a family of four would probably double the total global audience. Oddly, it is not the obscure shows that no-one cares about that demand a live audience, it is big name shows like *Strictly Come Dancing*. To watch all the excitement as it happens (yes, this is irony on my part), go along and register at **www. bbc.co.uk/showsandtours/tickets** – and have fun.

Think about changing your utility supplier.

You would have thought that the price of gas, water, electricity and a fixed phone line would be essentially the same whoever supplied the service. Oh, no. In the crazy world of deregulated utilities, thousands of folk are employed by various utility companies to persuade you to switch from one supplier to the next. So shop around and if you can strike a better deal, take it. You may say that this is all rather time-consuming and boring and you would be correct. So, declaring an interest (funds I manage own shares in this company), why not switch ALL your utilities (and that includes your mobile and internet) to **www.utilitywarehouse.co.uk** which will give you a discount for taking the whole package. Now, if you wish to go one stage further, you can sign up with this company to become a distributor and when you persuade your friends and neighbours to sign up as customers (so saving them money too), you gain a small commission paid each month to offset against your own bill – in theory you could actually make money out of this. Simple.

40

Invest in three plastic piggy banks (99p each at discount stores) and position them around the house.

Every time you walk past, put any coin worth 20p or less into them. Do not empty until they are full. You always end up losing small change – it falls through holes in your trousers or you toss it away to a street collector. But it adds up. My three piggy banks were emptied after eight months and yielded just under £120, 4 Euros and 2 US dollars. It all helps. As an aside, you might also start picking up coins you see lying on the street. There is a word for doing this which I cannot quite remember but it is surprisingly remunerative, especially in London where people appear to chuck money away with gay abandon. Of the £120 from my piggy banks collected in eight months, around £15 came from just picking up cash on the street – that is 40p a week. It may not sound a lot but it all adds up. 40p a week compounded over 20 years is £694.39.

41

Repay your mortgage early.

This is compound interest in reverse. Let us assume that your mortgage rate is 5% and that you are a basic rate taxpayer. Were you to invest £200 in an investment product to make £12 (a 6% return), after you have paid tax on that your return would be less than 5%. If you are a higher rate taxpayer at 50%, then you need to make £20 on your investment to generate a £10-after-tax return. Investing can be risky – certainly, to make a 10% return you have to accept that you may lose capital. But use that £200 to repay mortgage debt today and your saving is a guaranteed tax-free £10. And the way to effectively compound this is to ask your mortgage provider to maintain payments at the level they were before repayment. £200 compounded at 5% over 20 years is £530.66.

Put that another way: if you had a £100,000 mortgage repayable over 20 years, that one additional payment made in month one would reduce the term of your mortgage by five weeks. Now, were you to repay an additional £200 at the start of every year of your mortgage (you know you can afford it) and to maintain payments then you would (after just under 19 years) have reduced the capital outstanding by an additional £6,413.19, meaning that your mortgage would be paid off almost 16 months early. This is the simplest way for most homeowners to engage in risk-free, high-return saving.

42

Never buy designer labels.

Celebrities, and people who I have never heard of because I am too old and uncool but I am told are famous, are given designer labels to wear. Why do you think this is? Correct. It is because the owners of that label reckon that if Victoria Beckham is seen wearing it, the rest of womankind will rush out and buy it. Now, quite why anyone would want to follow the sartorial lead set by this particular intellectual heavyweight is beyond me, but there you go. Each to their own. But ask yourself, what is the real difference between a designer garment or accessory and a non-designer one? It is price. Who cares what folks think of you? It's your money.

To take this to the most base example, should I wish to purchase three pairs of Polo Ralph Lauren boxer shorts at John Lewis it will set me back £81. Should I instead buy a three-pack of John Lewis woven boxer shorts which will probably last as long and will be seen by two people (myself included) and a cat during their lifetime, it will set me back £17. What is the difference to me? You are correct: £64.

43

You cannot live without designer labels?
Okay, buy second hand.

Personally I think you are obsessed with image but that is your decision. At least stop blowing money by insisting on buying new. You can still be seen in designer labels but pay less by buying second hand. Obviously this does not apply to items such as the Polo Ralph Lauren boxer shorts referred to above but I suppose it could in theory. I digress. Charity stores will stock designer labels, especially in the more affluent areas, but you can also go online to websites such as **www.posh-swaps.com** where you can buy, sell or even swap a wide range of clothes including designer labels. Another good swap site can be found at **www.bigwardrobe.com**.

If you insist on going to the cinema check out the special offers.

Many cinemas offer 'early bird specials' – that is, cheap tickets to films in the morning which are unlikely to be packed out. You can get discounts of anywhere between 33% and 50% on such occasions. Some venues even have a cheap night once a week. If you are a customer of Orange you can of course take advantage of its 2-for-1 Wednesday night showing where you can bring along a friend for free. As I write, Orange is also offering a 2-for-1 deal with Pizza Express as part of this promotion and while that offer expires soon, one suspects it will be replaced with others in future. You can find more details on the Orange offers at **www.orange.co.uk**. You should also register with **www.seefilmfirst.com** which gives you the opportunity to watch free preview screenings of movies before they are released. Okay, you may end up watching a load of shockingly bad films but it is free!

45

Use supermarkets not corner stores.

I am afraid that this is not a popular thing to write, as people like having a friendly neighbourhood corner store which is open until 11 PM at night (well, about 7.30 PM here in the Isle of Man) run by that nice Mr Arkwright. It is a sentimental thing. But the reality is that these establishments simply cannot compete with the buying power and economies of scale offered by the supermarkets. If you are like my stepmother, you will go out of your way to support the small stores on principle because they are viewed (by her) as a community asset. In what way are they an asset? It is not that they offer greater choice than the supermarket. Nor is it that they offer better prices than the supermarket. Sometimes they are open later than the wicked supermarket but if Mr Jones the Greengrocer is feeling ill then his shop won't open until he recovers – Tesco always has staffing cover.

So in no sense are they a community asset other than in the sense that folks like my stepmother feel instinctively that they must fight against big corporations and stand shoulder to shoulder with the little guy. But the fact is that the 'community service' that the corner store provides is simply charging far more for basic foodstuffs and household goods than whichever wicked megacorp which runs the local supermarket. As such you should feel no qualms about helping to put the local corner store out of business by taking your trade to the supermarket. You will simply save money.

One handy tip on shopping for food. Never do it before you eat — that way you will find it easier to resist the temptation to impulse-buy a little snack just because you feel a bit peckish.

46

Take out redundancy insurance now. Or not at all.

Do not wait until you think that you might lose your job because it will be too late. Insurers will not pay out on such policies if you get a P45 and a black bin liner within six months of taking out protection. As such, if you think that it is inevitable that you are about to lose your job and do not have redundancy insurance (also know as unemployment insurance) then do not bother, as you won't collect a penny and are just wasting cash you will need on the premiums. But if you think that it is just possible that your job may be at risk – and in this climate that applies to most of us – but that there is nothing imminent, get insured so that if the worst happens you will have some income coming in even after you lose your job. Generally, you can get cover for 50-65% of your income up to around £2,000 pounds per month and this will last for a year after you lose your job. There are caveats as with all insurance but you should not wait until the threat looms large. Get cover now.

47

Get free dental treatment.

Dentist's bills are just ludicrous – right up there with the bills my cat's vet lands me with on a regular basis. But you can get treatment for free. Go to the website of the British Dental Association (**www.bda.org**) and look up details of Dental Universities who are seeking patients for their students to train on. Do not worry, each student working away on your molars is supervised by someone who is fully qualified and who can wade in to ensure that the correct tooth is removed and to assist if there is a minor mishap. But there shouldn't be. The dentists are only allowed to start practising on real live human volunteers after they have had extensive training elsewhere.

Incidentally, the same principle applies with acupuncture, should you wish to have needles stuck into various parts of your body. For more on that, go to the website of the British Acupuncture Council (**www.acupuncture.org.uk**). Good luck, and have fun.

48

Do not buy adult members of your extended family Christmas presents.

This does not mean that you are Scrooge, it is simply a recognition that you probably do not really know what your little sister wants for Christmas now that she is 39. Moreover, the issue of gifts exposes embarrassing questions based on the fact that different family members may now be far richer or poorer than their siblings. Do you really care if you get an extra jumper or an extra bottle of wine this Yuletide? I do not. For Christmas, the quantity of presents may matter (regrettably it probably does). But as adults, if we go through Christmas with the kids happy, putting on a few pounds, at least speaking to the wider family and avoiding too many rows over a heated stove with your partner (for whom you *should* get a present!) that is a great result. So, pre-agree a ceasefire on presents between the adult members of the wider family, well in advance so that you can all save a few quid and avoid any embarrassments later. For the avoidance of doubt, this year I shall send all my family a cracking good book which has recently been published and autographed by the author. They will also get the customary Yarg cheese – I choose to ignore my own rule, but make it clear that I want nothing in return. Adult Christmas presents really are a waste of money.

49

Take a mature approach to your partner's gift.

Make each other a stocking of little presents for when
you wake up, but why splash out on something dramatic
to leave under the tree? As a clumsy heterosexual male,
I know that whatever jewellery or clothes I buy will be a
hit or miss affair and I happily remember the year when
my partner and I each gave each other the same version
of Trivial Pursuit as one of the big gifts. Simply agree
what your budget is — it comes from the same pot ultimately — and buy something for the house or a romantic
weekend away for one of those dark February weekends.
If needs be, wrap the joint gift and unwrap it together
having left it underneath the tree on December 24th.

50

Cut down on or cut out after work drinks.

Journalism and the City, where I have spent my entire life, are heavy-duty drinking professions. But booze is clearly not good for your health and it is also incredibly expensive. It is an easy cost saving. In theory. In practice, I do not imagine that anyone reading this book will simply say 'Okay, I will drink less' and then stick to it. So perhaps the best that can be hoped for is to reduce the cost of your boozing.

If you have a student lifestyle and your aim on a Friday and Saturday night is to go out and get plastered, start drinking at the normal time but at home on cheaper take-aways from the supermarket and go out later. For grown ups fancying a Friday night 'one for the road', why not agree with your colleagues just to crack open a couple of bottles or a few cans at the end of the working week in the office. Not only do you avoid pub prices but there is a finite limit on how much you can drink – it's what you have pre-bought. The temptation to have 'just one more' is simply not there. The hard core may roll on from the office drinks to pub drinks but at least they have saved a few pounds. Most people having made the mental break of finishing a few social drinks with friends will then leave the office for home.

If you do end up in a bar, do not put your card behind the bar. You will simply lose track of what you are spending on booze and the temptation to add 'just another round' and to show unusual generosity is all the greater when you are not having to ferret around in your pocket for £20 notes each time you seek to quench the thirst of you and your colleagues. With your card behind the bar, the ability of those colleagues who historically do not 'stand their corner' to avoid paying their way becomes all the more evident. When you consider that the average Briton aged over 16 is spending £15 per week on alcohol (£780 a year), the scope to save a bit of cash in this department is very real.

Congratulations. You have made it to the half way point. You must by now have recognised numerous ways that you have been spending money needlessly. The first step is to recognise a way to save money. The second is to act on it. But before you start changing your finances for the better (and at this point you probably feel like a drink as you start to realise how much money you are wasting), there are another 51 handy hints to go. Read on...

51

Pay your insurance premiums in one go, not by monthly payments.

It might seem so much cheaper to pay over 12 months but it is not. This is in fact one of the more expensive forms of finance going, as you will be charged a premium of between 15% and 20% for doing so. That adds up. If you are paying £500 for home and car insurance (and I know that I pay a lot more) then you are probably paying £100 of that for the privilege of paying in instalments. So dig deep. Pay it all at the start of the year. And save yourself a ton of money.

52

Check all your bank statements
each month.

Do this for a year just as a reminder of all those direct
debts and standing orders that go out and you might have
forgotten about. That life membership of a society you
joined at University agreeing to pay £10 a year forever
– do you really still think you can be bothered? What
about that direct debit for £2.50 that goes out once a
month to some charity which you signed up for thanks
to an aggressive chugger on the street? Do you still like
that charity? Can you afford to support it even if you
do believe in what it does? You know that this is an easy
saving to be made.

Never pay to take cash out of a cash point machine or ATM.

Most bank ATMs will not charge you for withdrawing your own money. Hell, why should they? It is your money in the first place and the banks have saved a fortune by installing ATMs, since it has been calculated that for every two ATMs set up, the banks have been able to fire one employee working as a teller. But over the past few years a network of non-bank ATMs has grown up which charge around £1.85 per withdrawal. Now, even if you are taking out £200 a pop, that is still almost 1% of your cash being stolen by the machine. The average withdrawal from a charging ATM in the UK is just £46, which means that the machine operator is stealing 4% of the cash taken out – which is just ludicrous.

If you withdraw £50 a week from surcharging ATMs, you are wasting £96.20 a year – put another way, 50 of the withdrawals go to you and twice a year you take out the cash and hand it straight over to the ATM operator. Incidentally, when you pay £1.85, that money is split between the ATM operator and the owner of the site who, as often as not, is one of the corner store owners so beloved of my stepmother, providing a 'service to the community' by charging uncompetitive prices (see point 45).

If you insist on using surcharging ATMs, try taking out larger amounts less frequently. Taking out £100 twenty six times a year rather than £50 fifty two times a year will save you £48.10 a year. Better still, plan ahead and get cash out for free – use a bank ATM. Or use the cashback facility offered (for free) by those wicked supermarkets when you do your weekly shop. Your net saving should be at least £1-2 per week.

54

Never buy a new car, whatever generous terms the motor dealer offers you.

The value of your dream motor falls by 20% as soon as you drive it off the forecourt, as it then becomes a 'second hand motor, one careful owner.' It is quite simply the quickest way to destroy capital: you can send £2, £3 or £4,000 straight to money heaven in just minutes. Your ideal purchase is nearly new: someone who has sent his £4,000 off to money heaven but changed his mind a few months later. From that point onwards the depreciation (the fall in the resale value) is in a fairly straight line and reflects the real wear and tear and cost of keeping the car running in perfect order.

Always use the sales to do your shopping, but shop sensibly.

As a normal heterosexual male, I do not buy new shoes/suits/shirts/socks until the old ones really start to fall apart. As my old Dad taught me, there is no point replacing shoes until the holes in the soles are big enough for the water to come in and out of. Absolutely spot on: we Winnifriths save cash by not buying until everyone can see through the holes. Wrong: the policy of not buying until you face social embarrassment probably costs me several hundred pounds a year. The thing is that my various items of clothing fall apart at different times because they were bought at different times and disintegrate at different rates. So I end up wasting a lot of time. But far more importantly I end up wasting a lot of money. One organised trip a year to the January sales to buy a new pair of shoes, a new suit with two pairs of trousers and a dozen shirts will save me several hundred pounds given the discounts of 50% or more that I can obtain. For clothes, January is a good time for sales, although you can also get end-of-season bargains on summer lines in September as retailers seek to clear stock which will, at best, lie idle in their warehouses for another six months.

But do not buy in the sales what you do not need!

The temptation is all too real. You pay £150 for goods that would normally cost £350 – great, you have saved £200. But that saving is only a saving if you actually walk out of the stores without having actually spent the cash. Resist the urge to spend the additional £200 on clothes that you do not really need. You can kid yourself that you are better off because you have bought £700 worth of clothes for £350 but in cash terms your saving is precisely zippo. The aim of the saver is to increase the amount of cash you have/reduce your debts, not to increase the size of your wardrobe while your cash position remains unaltered.

Do not sign up to any get-rich schemes involving courses on anything from stock market success to sports betting or new franchise opportunities.

If the guy giving the course which will make you a millionaire from sports betting thinks it is such a sure-fire winner, why on earth would he let you in on the secret? Surely he would just be coining it in himself? The answer of course is that the only way to make a small fortune quickly is to start with a big fortune and gamble recklessly. There is no quick route to getting rich. Even the greatest investors only made it big over a long period. As such, anyone offering (for a small fee or often a large one) to help you get rich quick is basically a con artist and you should not offer him a penny. You may also be offered free courses on how to get rich quickly. Do not go on these either. Firstly nothing is free – trekking off to wherever the con artist is staging the course will incur travel and other costs and, secondly, once there you will almost certainly be charmed and pressurised into attending a 'master class' from the same conman which will not be free. The free course was just a way of luring you into his lair so that he could get you to part with your cash later. Since his offers will be tempting and his (commission driven) salesmen will be tenacious, put yourself out of risk and just do not attend any get-rich-quick courses.

58

On the other hand, always enter free competitions.

They are free and the odds of winning are very long indeed but if you have time on your hands and the cost of entry is nil then if you enter enough competitions you might win something. The internet is jam-packed with websites where you can register for free and then just enter competition after competition: there are so many websites to choose from that I just suggest you do a Google search restricted to the UK for 'free competitions'.

59

Sign up to take part in online market research.

This can be done quickly and from home on your PC. The leading site for this is IPSOS (**www.iap-inter-active.com**) where you will normally be allowed to take part in four member surveys a month, which will reward you with points which tally up over time and can be redeemed for vouchers at stores such as Boots, Amazon, John Lewis and IKEA. The IPSOS programme also enters all its survey participants in a number of free draws where you can win a car, a big holiday or simply cash. The odds of winning one of those draws are long but it does not cost you anything to enter. If you are feeling a bit more adventurous, you can sign up to become a panellist in studio-based market research focus groups.

Register with sites such as **www.claret-uk.com** and **www.sarosresearch.com** – this is not a full time job but you can earn anything between £30 and £100 for two hours of your time. You should also be able to stuff your face with crisps, twiglets and a range of other snacks and drinks provided by the market research company. So view this as being paid to have a free meal.

60

Make sure that you have a loyalty card for each supermarket you use.

Before my stepmother points it out, I am aware that the objective of store cards is to enable Big Brother Megacorp to track every purchase you make so that it can send you promotional offers designed to ensure that you buy yet more of its products. But do I really care if Tesco knows that I am a regular purchaser of cat food and cat litter? If it means that my store card will save me money when I next buy cat food that is great. And if that means that Tesco sends me promotions offering even greater discounts on cat food going forward, that is even better. So always ensure that you have a store card for every supermarket that you use regularly.

61

Never buy an additional extended warranty on an electrical product.

You will be covered anyway for the first couple of years and the odds are that if your TV or DVD player lasts that long, it will be good for another couple of years when the warranty expires anyway. The real cost of electrical goods is falling so fast that the odds are that your replacement cost when the TV or DVD breaks will be far lower than today's price. The electrical stores companies make a mint on such products which are, in reality, just incredibly high-cost insurance. The salesmen who try to flog you them are not doing so for your financial well being. Moreover, claiming under such a policy is such a time-consuming process that you will find it far less stressful (and almost certainly cheaper) not to buy and simply to replace the goods when they break which will – almost certainly – be after the extended warranty would have expired anyway.

62

Book your flights early.

In two days I will fly from the Isle of Man to London and, as I booked only last week, I will touch down at City Airport £169 poorer. Doing a bit of forward planning, I looked at booking the same flight for three months' time and the cost was almost £100 less. The reason is simple. The airlines want to know as far in advance as possible that they have covered their fixed costs. So if they can sell 80% of their seats at, say, £70, and know that the flight is going to break even months in advance, they are delighted. They can then rack the prices up dramatically for the remaining seats knowing that any seat sales they do make are pure profit. And thus disorganised suckers (like me this week) who have no choice but to book a seat whatever the price, provide all the profit. So plan ahead and get a cheap seat to help the airline break even. Or be a disorganised sucker, pay a huge premium and help the airline make a huge profit. It is your call. It is now August. Those who plan ahead are booking their winter tickets now. Incidentally, the same principle applies to train fares.

If you are going on a short-haul or even medium-haul flight, take a packed lunch.

Or buy your sandwiches and a drink once in the airport but when you have passed through security (otherwise fluids over 100 ml in size will be confiscated). The price of airport food is bad enough but the price you pay for plastic food once in the air is ludicrous. It is bad enough that the contents taste just the same as the packaging but the prices charged are usurious. A general rule of cost saving: never buy anything on an aeroplane.

64

If you are planning to drive to the airport, think well in advance about where you will park.

The closer to the airport you plan to leave your car, the more expensive it is to park. Is it worth allowing an extra half an hour's travel time in order to save £50 in car parking fees? Almost certainly, yes. It is also worth searching ahead and pre-booking car park spaces. At some airports this may not be practical but at places such as Manchester a pre-booked slot for a week can cost less than £30. If you plan to hire a car at the airport you are arriving at do not wait until you get there and never take the 'special offer' pushed on you by the airline, as that will simply push you into the longest queue. Book a car hire well ahead over the internet to get the best rates and do not book that car hire via an airline website as that will not save you money. Book it as a stand-alone item.

65

Don't buy a turkey at Christmas.

I have never understood the appeal of this bird: it is incredibly hard work to keep moist and it does not really taste that good. But it is tradition, so we carry on, year in year out, going for boring old turkey. By the day after Boxing Day as you are still working your way through an increasingly dry old carcass thinking of the next variant on how to spice it up (Coronation Turkey anyone?) you really are wondering: why, oh why? Why indeed? The shops/poultry producers see you coming and in December turkey really is a pretty pricey bird for something that tastes so bland. Dare to be different. Go for a leg of lamb. Continue to have all the vegetables and Christmas pudding and all the booze as per normal but why not save a few quid on the centrepiece and eat something you actually like? If you insist on turkey, do not buy one that is bigger than you really need – 1lb (0.5 kilogrammes) per person will easily suffice. Remember: it is turkey, no one will be asking for seconds.

As an aside, think about those on their own at Christmas. It is pretty lonely for them and also expensive making a meal for one if they can be bothered. So think of a lonesome friend, neighbour or relative and invite them round. Perhaps even invite a couple without kids. The odds are that they will contribute in some way – usually on the booze front if you choose wisely – and so they will more than pay their own way. So do a good and kind thing at Christmas and save money too!

Recycle your Christmas tree.

Every year I buy a tree at Columbia Road in London and every year there is a different reason why Christmas tree inflation had galloped ahead whatever is happening in the rest of the economy: too much snow in Norway, a new bug that has arrived from Canada which eats Christmas trees only, new *elf n safey* regulations on chopping down trees which have added to the cost, not enough snow in Norway. It doesn't matter, the price always goes up. And I always put my back out lugging the tree home. This is all such a waste of time and money. If you have a garden, buy a tree with roots and put it in a big earth-filled tub just a few days before Christmas. Feed and water it well and then on the 12th day of Christmas, take it back outside and gently put it back in the garden where it should recover, grow a few inches, and be ready for another ordeal in 12 months' time. One day it will get too big for the house and you will have to buy it a little brother and start the whole process all over again. Having a live tree also reduces the amount of pine needles which drop in your carpet. If you have no garden, consider an artificial tree. Absolutely no danger of pine needles dropping and by the time you have covered it with decorations, angel's hair and tinsel it is hard to know the difference.

Always use price comparison websites.

Whether it is holidays or perfumes or bicycles or insurance, the principle is the same: always use price comparison websites to check out where you can buy exactly the same goods at the cheapest price. For perfumes have a look at **www.cheapperfumeexpert.com**, for holidays have a look at **www.travelsupermarket.com** and for airline tickets have a look at **www.cheapflights. co.uk** – in fact if you want to buy almost anything there are a plethora of websites for each industry offering you a multitude of options and allowing you to buy the cheapest one. From the comfort of your own room, saving money has never been simpler.

68

Start a pension as soon as you begin work.

There are two reasons why it is criminal NOT to do this. The first is that the Government will gross up your contributions at the basic rate of tax, so if you make a pension contribution of just £8 a month (I am rounding up here to make my maths simpler) the Government will gross that up to £10. So you are being paid to save. This is free money. (Okay, it comes out of taxes you have already paid but it is madness not to take it.) And then we come back to that old point of compounding. Every year that money sits in your pension pot is another year that it is generating a return and the next year, not only does your original investment (topped up by the grateful taxpayer) earn an investment but so does the prior year's return on investment. The difference in the pension pot you eventually get on retirement between someone starting a pension at 22 or 32 or 42 (you have left it very late if you start at 42) is startling. The latest you should start a pension is 30. If you are smart, you start the day that you begin work and paying taxes.

69

Grandparents should, for Christmas presents, always consider handing down family momentos, the family silver or other treasured possessions.

There are three reasons for this. The most laudible one is that it will provide a treasured link for your children and grandchildren to generations gone by. So as I write, looking down sternly on me is a portrait of my great grandfather who was – as it happens – a herald, so is wearing a colourful sort of dress. He still looks stern. He also looks like my father which makes me rather worry what I shall look like in 30 years' time. The second reason to do this is that the cash cost of such a gift is nil. And as such you save money. And the final reason is that if the memento or heirloom actually has a tangible value then – assuming that the grandparent can live for another seven years – this gift has fallen outside the scope of capital gains tax. Frankly, even if the grandparent does not last seven years, you can probably avoid declaring it as part of the estate and so escape the CGT net anyway. With house prices having risen so sharply in the past decade, a surprising number of folks will find that there is CGT payable on their estates and anything you can do to reduce that liability now seems like a good idea. After all CGT is in fact a tax on wealth built up on the basis of income that has already been taxed. What is wrong in reducing the amount one has to pay in this double tax?

If you have a garden, try growing some of your own food.

My late mother was a great believer in the self sufficiency movement so beloved of '60s and '70s people with long hair and beards. (For the record: my mother did not have a beard, that was just the men.) So I was brought up growing our own food, picking food from hedgerows, making our own elderflower champagne and even nettle beer. I do not expect many people to go that far, although I made elderflower wine again a couple of years ago and it was actually quite good fun and a cheap way to keep the family entertained for a day (picking the flowers, mixing the champagne and then eventually bottling). It tasted dreadful but that is another matter. However, even the smallest garden can be quite productive and buying a few packs of seeds is an awful lot cheaper than buying the finished goods in a supermarket.

Gardening is also a healthy and relaxing way to exercise and homegrown fresh food tastes so much better than refined supermarket produce. If you do not have a garden you can try to get a Council allotment but be warned there are, in most places, quite long waiting lists to secure your little plot of land. Is it worth it financially? Yes it is. One study in the US showed that an ordinary sized garden ($1/25^{th}$ of an acre) could for an investment of £100 in seeds and manure (mostly manure and you can probably cut the cost of this if you live in the countryside or if you are an MP and can claim it on expenses) produced a yield of approximately £1500 worth of fruit and vegetables. You can of course increase your yields by picking up produce from hedgerows. My mother was right all along.

Do NOT join a gym after Christmas because you feel fat.

You will lose pounds but only financial ones. The gyms always demand a joining fee of one month's membership and more than a third of those who join a gym in January are using it rarely or never by the time that the Easter eggs are dished out. So two months membership at £40 a month will actually end up costing you £60 a month. You will also, in the majority of cases, be locked into a 12-month contract, losing yourself even more money. In fact...

72

If hint number 71 comes too late for you, quit your gym now.

Buy some strong running shoes (one month's membership) or a second hand bike (two month's membership) and hit the roads. You will save additional amounts by not having to rent a towel or feeling the urge to buy an energy drink after your workout. If you are really ambitious you can purchase a rowing machine at Tesco's and have it delivered to your house for just over three month's membership. And as an added bonus you do not have to put up with all those superfit people running twice as fast as you without breaking into a sweat and looking condescendingly at you as you struggle vainly to appear not quite as out of shape as you are.

When you use a washing machine,
use it on the lowest heat.

Ninety degrees is – with the advent of modern washing powders – just a complete waste of money. Sixty degrees should only be used for nappies and heavily soiled bed clothes. As such you should store up such items (in a sealed carrier bag for obvious reasons) and do such a wash only once a week. Most folks used to wash at fifty degrees when cleaning polyester/cotton mixtures, nylon, cotton and viscose but modern washing powders contain enzymes which mean that you can achieve just the same results at forty degrees. Frankly, for most regular washes (obviously not white cotton shorts or very dirty items) you will not go wrong even on a thirty-degree wash. The energy and the cost savings are material.

74

Do not bother to use extra energy with a spin dry programme.

And do not use a tumble dryer – which guzzles electricity – if you have within your house or flat, room for a clothes horse or – in the summer months – a clothes line. A typical tumble dryer costs about 24p an hour to run so for a family using it twice a week that is 50p (or £26 a year) completely wasted.

75

Flog your unwanted possessions on eBay.

Are you sure that you need or wanted everything kicking
around your house? I am pretty sure that I do not. I will
deal with my old REO Speedwagon cassette later in hint
number 84 but if I root through the assorted packing
cases of books and other junk collected over the years
and now lying unopened here in the Isle of Man, then
there just have to be things that I do not want or do not
need. That the cases have remained unopened for six
months is testimony to the latter point. So sell this junk
and use the cash to reduce your most expensive debts or
– if you have no debt at all – to put into a tax free savings
wrapper (hint 92 – see below). The simplest way to get
rid of your unwanted goods is to put them up for sale on
eBay **www.ebay.co.uk,** thereby tapping into a global
audience of junk (sorry bargain) hunters. I am told by
eBay addicts that you should not put the whole attic up
for sale at once. Instead put one item up for sale, sell it
and ensure that it is delivered. Then repeat the process.
That way you will build up a track record as a trusted
seller which will mean that other folks are more likely to
buy your goods as the disposal process proceeds.

Right. Almost three quarters of the way there. If you have not spotted more than a dozen ways to transform your personal finances I shall eat my hat. Well, that is a lie. I do not have a hat, hat's do not – I suspect – taste very good and, above all, it would be a waste of money as hats are far more expensive than a good meal of own-label baked beans. But you get my drift.

When you are going abroad, let your friends know and ask them to text rather than phone.

You pay around £9 an hour to receive calls in Europe and up to £60 an hour elsewhere in the world, but receiving texts is free. Texting back costs around 11p per text in the EU and up to 40p elsewhere but it is a heck of a lot cheaper than calling. Better still, switch your mobile off when abroad so no-one can rack up big bills for you and just check once a day for urgent messages. If you have a Blackberry or other data-transferring device and plan a trip or holiday, just switch it off. The work world can live without you. No really, it can.

When the weather starts to get colder (around August 29ᵗʰ here in the Isle of Man) do not automatically turn up the heating.

My method of clamping down on heating bills is just to stay late in the heated office and then go home and straight to bed before I notice how cold my house is. But I accept that for those who want to have a life or who have a family to think about this may not be a viable option.

However, before you rush to hike up the thermostat (which heats the whole house, most of which you are not using) try putting on more clothes: extra socks, a vest and perhaps a woolly jumper or two. At least try it and see how long you can hold out for! Put an extra quilt on the bed rather than bringing an electric heater (power guzzler) into your room. Consider investing in a hot water bottle (these can be bought for as little as £3.75 with free delivery at **www.hotwaterbottle.org. uk**).

Do not use the scoops provided by manufacturers of detergents for your washing machine.

They are not sized at optimum levels. Well, not for you anyway. The aim of the scoops is to encourage you to use more detergent so that you buy more. You can get away with using only half a scoop without affecting the quality of your weekly wash.

79

Do not boil a full kettle.

Just boil enough to make one cup of tea (or two if you have a friend round). This might sound like penny pinching but it adds up. Most kettles are about 3000watts and take about four minutes to boil if full. Electricity is about 12p per unit, so your kettle takes about 36p per hour, four minutes is 1/15 of an hour, so 36 divided by 15 is 2.4p to boil a full kettle. If you boil just enough water for your cuppa the cost falls to 0.4p. The average Briton drinks just over 1000 cups of tea per annum so for your average Brit boiling only enough water for one cuppa rather than boiling a full kettle each time they want a cuppa, the saving runs to £20 a year.

If you shop online, use promotional codes.

Go to **www.myvouchercodes.co.uk** where you can register for free to receive the weekly newsletter with the latest offers or you can browse to get all the offers already running. The idea is that the stores who participate get to whip up extra trade to clear surplus stock – but also by offering special promotions they get you to buy more. But you are too disciplined to fall for those traps. You simply browse the store when you wish to purchase a specific item to see if there is a discount offer on that item. You will be able to access a special promotional code when buying that item online and then get a discount. Hey presto. It is that simple. But remember to be disciplined. Do not be tempted to buy what you do not need just because there is a discount. Only use this to get a discount on something you planned to buy anyway.

Do not buy ready made meals.

Even if they are endorsed by Delia, Jamie, Gordon or that fat posh bloke with the beard whose face looks as if it has been squashed by a sausage machine. Not only are their health benefits uncertain relative to home cooked food but they are also hugely expensive when compared to preparing you own food from scratch. With the average UK family spending £200 per month on food and drink it is estimated that preparing your own meals rather than boosting the already bloated bank balances of Delia, Jamie, Gordon and the fat posh bloke with a beard could save you around £25 a month.

82

Cut down on the meat.

Now this might be a step too far but meat is far more expensive than vegetables and you can cut down on your intake. For instance, when you make pasta Bolognese, just cut out the meat and add some flavouring to the tomato sauce. Stir fries also cut out the meat with the flavours from the soy sauce and the oils infusing the vegetables in such a way that you almost do not notice that you are eating rabbit food. Cut out meat from three family meals a week and your annual saving will be around £300. I should stress that I have no intention of doing this myself as rabbit always tastes far better than rabbit food but I offer it up as a suggestion for those of a less carnivorous nature.

83

Do not let food go off.

It goes without saying that the cardinal rule for saving money on food is not to let it go off and go to waste. So if you are not using food instantly, put it in the freezer. If you sense that food is approaching its use-by date, then use it. I refer back to that stir fry – you can put anything into a stir fry, meat, vegetables, fish, old socks, the cat. Just add the soy sauce and it all tastes pretty much the same (of soy sauce) and so the stir fry is a great way to create a cheap meal and use up foodstuffs approaching their sell-by date. Pasta is a good purchase in this respect since it more or less lasts forever and so will never go to waste. I should stress that I was only kidding about putting the cat in a stir fry but I am sure that really old socks would just blend in.

84

Make some money out of those old Cliff Richard and Brotherhood of Man CDs.

All CDs have a value, even those produced by the Brotherhood of Man. We all have CDs we regret buying and wished we had not purchased and will never listen to again. That REO Speedwagon compilation* I bought to impress Abbe Aronson does not deserve to be heard by anyone and surely I must have been drunk when I snapped up *The Smurfs Christmas Hits*? But they are not worthless. Well, they are in musical terms truly worthless but amazingly they have a monetary value. Simply go to **www.musicmagpie. co.uk** and type in the bar code and, hey presto, you will be paid money for something you will never, ever want to hear again. Incidentally this website will also give you hard cash for DVDs (even the appalling *Green Street 2* which I ordered when drunk) and video games.

*I admit that the REO Speedwagon compilation was in fact an old fashioned device called a cassette and so it is, I am afraid, just worthless. It is a function of my age that I own cassettes. I will not seek money for the REO Speedwagon cassette. It deserves only one fate – burning. I do hope Abbe's taste in music has improved since 1985.

85

You can also realise cash for old mobile phones.

The sums involved here are staggering – real telephone numbers. In the UK alone there are around 20 million handset upgrades each year. Why, I do not know, but then I am a bit of a Luddite and have changed my phone only twice in 10 years. The average UK household now has four unused mobiles sitting around the house doing nothing. And they can all be turned into cash. Go to websites such as **www.mazumamobile.com** or **www. sellmymobile.com** and they will give you hard cash for your duff old handset.

The corporate spin on these operations is that they are stopping toxic substances leaking into the environment or even sending old phones off to poor people in Africa and Asia so that they can text each other. I am almost crying with happiness as I search out the two non-used phones in this house to help some poor starving Africans. The willingness of these companies has nothing whatsoever to do with the fact that most handsets will be stripped down to extract valuable Nickel, Lithium, Gold, other metals and plastics and that they will make a stack of cash as a result. No. Nothing at all. It is all about helping poor starving Africans. Whatever. The bottom line is that you can find those four useless handsets hidden in the back of your sofa or behind the cat's litter tray, put them in a freepost envelope and get hard cash back almost instantaneously.

Conversely, you are probably entitled to a free upgrade to your mobile every 12/18/24 months dependent on the level of contract. You should always take the upgrade to the sexiest and latest phone and immediately sell it on eBay for a premium price whilst continuing to use your old brick of a mobile – new handsets regularly fetch over £200 when sold. This may be a bit dodgy but everyone seems to do it.

86

Complete and prepare to submit your tax return as soon as possible.

This may sound like insanity but hang on. You might just be lucky and discover that, after filling in all those complex boxes and doing your sums, that you are entitled to a tax rebate – many thousands of people are each year. In which case, send the form back as soon as you can after the end of the tax year and await a cheque from the Inland Revenue. If you find – as most of us sadly do – that you owe the taxman money then there is also no real point in delaying submitting the return (the deadline is October 31st in paper format or January 31st online) as you will have the same deadline to pay either way – 31st January in the year after the end of the prior tax year. If you are partially or fully self employed spend an hour with an accountant (itself tax deductible) to ensure that you claim every cost you can against tax in order to minimise your obligations. There is no point delaying the payment of tax after January 31st as you will be automatically fined for doing so.

87

If your pet passes away, don't replace him/her/it.

Owning a cat or dog, let alone something more exotic, is quite simply very expensive. Food, vet bills, passports, holiday care, vaccinations, presents at Christmas (Kitosh always gets a Christmas present!), cages for transporting, flea powder, vetinarary care insurance, a decent burial plot (Okay, that is optional): it stacks up. The average cost of owning a cat or dog over its lifetime is estimated at £6,000-£10,000. Of course my cat is worth it and I do not begrudge him a penny but that is an awful lot of cash. If you assume that a cat or dog lives for 10 years then over 25 years the average UK homeowner could clear one quarter of their mortgage (assuming the savings are paid in every month and compounded at 5%) – without making any changes to their other spending habits simply by not owning a pet.

88

Cut out or cut down on the number of times you eat out.

The restaurant will be making a 70% margin on the food it serves you, at least the same again on drink it plies you with and an almost 90% margin on every cup of coffee it persuades you to order. And then it adds a service charge on top. It is a truly expensive way to meet your daily calorific requirements and you know it. Yes, it is a pleasurable experience but it is also a luxury that you can easily cut out. Invite friends round for supper instead with you sharing out courses to prepare. It is so much cheaper and you do not need to appoint a designated driver afterwards.

89

Do not use taxis ever – use public transport.

It is far cheaper to travel by bus or underground (especially if you bulk-buy tickets with an Oystercard in London). It is more environmentally friendly and given the congestion on the roads it is probably at least as quick. But it is the cash element that really matters – stop using taxis for a month and stick a tenner into a pot every time you use public transport where you would formerly have used a cab and see how much you have saved at the end of the four weeks. Try this experiment once and you will never flag a cab again.

90

Use the January sales to buy kids' birthday party presents in advance.

One of the truly horrific things about the modern kids' birthday party is the expectation that when your little darling goes to a party she has to take a small gift. And when she (or he) hosts his or her own birthday party you also have to provide a small gift bag for all the little horrors who attend. It was all different in my day but there you go. The thing is that all these little darlings do not really appreciate this multiplicity of tiny little gifts, it is just one of those niceties of modern etiquette. So bulk buy a year's supply of these useless trinkets that will be discarded within days of receipt in the January sales. Store and then use as needed.

If you are truly desperate for cash, then loan your body to medical science.

Go to **www.gpgp.net** to discover about medical trials
on new drugs for which you can be a human guinea
pig. You do not have to be ill, pharmaceutical companies also seek out fit and healthy volunteers to act as
human guinea pigs to see if their products are safe. Aha:
I think you realise the downside. But before we come
to that, you will get paid and you might even get free
food and accommodation if you are lucky. Now to the
downside. The drugs will all have been tested on animals
but, as you might be aware, animals can react differently
to humans and what might have no effect on a cat or a
mouse could kill you or cause serious side effects. The
odds are against it but this is not something I would rec-
ommend to anyone with a family to support or indeed
who is not well and truly desperate for cash. The phrase
'last resort' springs to mind.

If you have cleared all your debts and are ready to save, use an ISA (and Individual Savings Allowance).

An ISA is not a savings product in itself but is a tax wrapper. Each adult can set up one ISA a year and anything earned on the savings within that ISA is exempt from tax – be it interest, dividends or even capital gains. You can invest up to £10,200 in an ISA each year and that number will rise with inflation. Of that amount, you can put up to £5,100 on a cash ISA where your capital will be protected and you just earn (tax free) interest. The rest of your allowance can be invested in most shares and all unit trusts so even the risk-averse should be able to find a shares-linked product (a blue chip or FTSE 100 high-yield fund) to suit their needs. You can close down your ISA and take out the cash at any time. The bottom line is that anyone who has cash and thinks that leaving it in a bank account is sensible saving is just mad, as the taxman will be taking a good slice (basic rate income tax) away from the interest you earn. The taxman cannot touch what is inside your ISA. So you should – if you have spare cash – use your maximum ISA allowance (a husband and wife have one each) every tax year, which starts on April 6th.

Incidentally, if you are investing in either equities or Unit Trusts in your ISA I suggest that you do so via 12 equal monthly payments rather than in one lump sum. And that is because the value of investments will go up and down as the year progresses. You might get lucky with your one lump sum investment and buy at the year low. Or you might get unlucky and buy at the year high. So it is better to drip your cash in over the course of the whole year and average out the cost of purchase.

Mr Muscle, Vim and all those expensive sprays and squeezy bottles packed full of chemicals for cleaning your house are a complete waste of money.

Do not buy another bottle ever again. To clean a surface just as effectively as an expensive supermarket cream use a teaspoon of bicarbonate of soda on a damp cloth (just like my mum used to) – it works just as well. When you are tackling the sorts of surfaces that you need to be smear-free, such as windows, mirrors and bathroom surfaces, ordinary vinegar does the trick. So when your supermarket-bought squeezy bottle is empty, replace it with a mixture of water (three parts) and ordinary vinegar (cheapest own label purchase) – one part will be perfect. And much cheaper. I am also told that bicarbonate of soda can be used as a deodorant or (with salt) as a cheap alternative to toothpaste. I cannot say that I have been brave enough to try out these two money-saving ideas.

Cut down on the number of TV channels you pay for on Sky.

Do you honestly watch all the channels you pay for? Are there some which you watch so infrequently that the added cost of having them on your package really does not stack up? Is it really worth being on a more expensive package just so that you can watch a channel once or twice a year? Cut down to the basic package and use the money you bank each month on a real treat. You could easily save £20 a month and what you are not watching you won't really miss.

You can get extra entertainment for free at your local library.

These days libraries do not just stock books but DVDs and those ghastly computer games so beloved by the younger generation. So do not go and buy new books/DVDs/computer games, just join the library and as long as you return them on time the service is essentially free. The library is another reason not to pay to join DVD rental services such as LoveFilm – DVD rental is cheaper in libraries than via a commercial service and for OAPs it is usually free. It might be simpler to have DVDs posted to you or to pay to watch new movies come out on Sky but it is a total waste of money. Stop being so lazy and watch the savings mount up.

96

Get your hair cut for free.

Hairdressers seem to charge almost as much as dentists and vets for their services. I often think that I am in the wrong job but I guess that there are a lot of reasons why I would make an unconvincing hairdresser. And as for the places dentists and vets have to stick their fingers... maybe they have every right to charge what they do. Anyhow, it is possible to get your hair cut for free or (at worst) for a minimal charge and that is to volunteer to have it cut by a student. Even upmarket saloons such as Toni & Guy and Vidal Sassoon have students who need victims (I mean customers) to practice on. And there are numerous colleges of higher education throughout the UK offering courses in hairdressing. They all need hair to cut. I am sure that you know the risk but if it does not work you can always go back to your normal place and pay the full whack to get your hair back in the style you like. Be aware you will need to make an appointment at a time to suit the students but if you want to save money that – and the small risk of looking like Lord Blackadder – is the price you pay.

Do not bother with a hotel when going on holiday.

The really frugal may opt for a 'staycation' so avoiding all the unpleasantness of travel, being stuck in airports for hours due to volcanic ash, and all the family rows that this entails – the cheapest holiday you will ever enjoy. Just put your feet up. Do not go to work. Watch a (rigged) cricket match on the TV, drink and eat too much and think of all the money you are saving. Okay, you want a change. I understand that. But oddly enough, so do folks living in places where you may wish to go on holiday. So why not go for a home swap. You can find details of how to do this on websites such as **www. homeforexchange.com** and **www.homeexchange. com** as well as many others.

Incidentally, if you live in London, with the 2012 Olympics looming you may well be in for a treat. And I do not refer to the sight of dozens of corrupt third world rulers being driven in chauffeur driven limousines through the capital to watch hundreds of drug-primed athletes cheat their way to Olympic glory in sports in which you or I will never have any interest whatsoever. The treat is that there are tens of thousands of folk around the world who really are interested in the Olympic games and who will be desperate for accommodation in London. Since all the hotels will be full of the afore-mentioned third world tyrants, these ordinary Olympic-anoraks will be wanting to rent flats and houses and will be paying daft prices. The evidence from prior Olympics is that you should start to look to rent out your place as soon as possible as rental prices fall if you hang on to the last minute hoping for a really daft offer. So rent your place out and go sit on a Greek beach for four weeks and come back still 'in the money'. On the same track: let us hope that England wins the World Cup 2018 bid and we can all go and watch the national team fail miserably once again from the comfort of a bar in the Med.

Stop using 0870 or 0871 numbers.

These are effectively premium rates but are not advertised as such. Even calling from a land line you could well be paying 10p per minute and that cash is not going to BT (well, a bit of it is) but is largely ending up in the pocket of those you call: companies such as Comet, Barclaycard and Vodafone who probably have rather more cash than you do at the start of the process. Why on earth should you make them even richer when you are probably calling with a legitimate customer service issue anyway? There is an answer. Go to **www. saynoto0870.com** where you should be able to find an alternative landline number allowing you to make the same call. Saving 20p or 30p might not sound like much but the added pleasure that you are depriving companies such as Barclays of an extra bit of – totally underserved – profit makes it all worth while.

99

Stop buying bottled water.

If you are not happy to drink tap water – and that is understandable – then invest in a water filter jug. The cheapest model going can be bought from Amazon for less than £12 with free delivery and one cartridge. Cartridges – which have to be replaced every 500 litres – are extra. Six (which should last for at least a year) will set you back another £22. That should be enough to deliver you 2000 litres of purified clean water for a total outlay of £34 – or 1.7p a litre. Go to a shop and a six-pack of 1.5 litre still water (i.e. nine litres) will set you back £2.50 (27.8p per litre). It is a no-brainer for those who insist on 'clean' water. A final hint: if you are out shopping or going to the gym, take water with you as it is a complete waste of money to buy additional (expensive) water when out, which you can produce at home for just 1.7p per litre.

100

Do not pay bills late.

You might think that you are saving money but you are not – you are merely adding to the pain, albeit on a deferred basis, as those to whom you owe money will without hesitation slap fines and exorbitant rates of interest on you. Of course there is no need to pay early, as soon as a bill arrives. Why should your hard-earned cash sit in the bank account of a major utility or the Government (rather than in your own bank account) for any longer than is needed? So wait until the last moment you can pay within the deadline and then pay. If you really cannot afford to pay a bill then do not just sit there and hope that it will go away because, I am afraid, it will not. 'Fess up as soon as you know that you cannot pay to the utility in question and explain the reason for your hardship. If it is genuine you may be presented with a payment plan which avoids fines or being cut off.

101

Stop buying lottery tickets.

The odds are that you will not win. The odds on you
winning the jackpot are 14 million to 1. The odds of you
being struck by lightning are a mere 3 million to 1. If
you were to invest £14,000 a week your odds would still
be 1,000 to 1 against a win. By definition, you need a
vast number of non winners to pay for a) the winner, b)
the administration costs and c) the money the Lottery
gives to 'good causes'. If you invest £2 a week in lottery
tickets for 20 years you will almost certainly not win the
jackpot – your odds are 6,730 to 1 against. On the other
hand if you put that £2 a week into a sensible savings plan
and generate a 5% compound return you will end up
with £3,610.81. And that is guaranteed.

By now you should already be feeling much, much richer. Whatever the recession throws at you and your family, you are now fully armed to save money, to generate extra cash quickly without any risk or outlay and to prosper while others suffer. Good luck. We are all going to need it in the years that lie ahead. And if there is no recession? Well why not save money that you would have otherwise wasted anyway?

Acknowledgements

Acknowledgements

I should like to thank Simon Petherick and his team at Beautiful Books for commissioning this work. And all my colleagues at Rivington Street Holdings for coming up with so many helpful suggestions, notably the psycho trader John Piper, Siobhra Murphy, Martin Greenwood, Fungai Ndoro and especially Ross Jones for all his support. Thank you also to Karen Castaneda and Richard Gill for their helpful suggestions which although amusing were all also totally illegal and so did not make the final cut. Or indeed the first one.

Thanks to the board and senior managers of Rivington Street Holdings (Jim, Denham, Mike, Russell and Nick) for their support in completing this book as so much else was juggled, to my father for his unswerving love and support in so many ways over the years (which really is appreciated and is not forgotten), to Monny for the Tailor of Gloucester analogy and much else and finally to Kitosh for providing someone to talk to as I worked late into the night to complete this volume (almost) on time. Kitosh: please ignore hint 87 – I would not even consider it for a moment.